U.S. PRESIDENTS

Franklin D. Roosevelt. John F. Kennedy. Ronald Reagan.

THREE EXTRAORDINARY LEADERS

By the Editors of TIME FOR KIDS

BACKPACKBOOKS

○

NEW YORK

Franklin D. Roosevelt © 2006 by Time Inc.
John F. Kennedy © 2005 by Time Inc.
Ronald Reagan © 2006 by Time Inc.

This 2007 edition published by Backpack Books
by arrangement with HarperCollins Publishers Inc.

ISBN-13: 978-1-4351-0112-8
ISBN-10: 1-4351-0112-X

Printed and bound in China.

1 3 5 7 9 10 8 6 4 2

About the Author of FRANKLIN D. ROOSEVELT: Jeremy Caplan, a former editor at
TIME FOR KIDS®, is currently a reporter for TIME magazine. A graduate of the Woodrow
Wilson School at Princeton University, he is an avid violinist, athlete, and cook. The author
lives in New York City.

Copyright © by Time Inc.

TIME FOR KIDS and the Red Border Design are Trademarks of Time Inc. used under license.

Photography and Illustration Credits:
Cover: Bettmann–Corbis; cover inset: Time Life Pictures–Getty Images; cover flap: Atlanta Historical Society; title page: Corbis; contents page:
Bettmann–Corbis; p.iv: Time Life Pictures–Getty Images; p.2: Bettmann–Corbis; p.3: Bettmann–Corbis; p.4: AP Photo; p.5: Franklin D. Roosevelt
Presidential Library & Museum; p.6: Franklin D. Roosevelt Presidential Library & Museum; p.7: Franklin D. Roosevelt Presidential Library & Museum;
p.8: Franklin D. Roosevelt Presidential Library & Museum; p.9 (top): Jim McKnight–AP Photo; p.9 (bottom): Franklin D. Roosevelt Presidential Library
& Museum; p.10: courtesy of Groton School; p.11: Franklin D. Roosevelt Presidential Library & Museum; p.12: Franklin D. Roosevelt Presidential Library
& Museum; p.13: Franklin D. Roosevelt Presidential Library & Museum; p.14: Franklin D. Roosevelt Presidential Library & Museum; p.15: Corbis;
p.16: Franklin D. Roosevelt Presidential Library & Museum; p.17: AP Photo; p.18: Legacy Historical Antiques; p.19: UPI; p.20: courtesy of FDR's
Little White House, Georgia Dept. of Natural Resources; p.21: Franklin D. Roosevelt Presidential Library and Museum; p.22: AP Photo; p.23:
Hulton Archive–Getty Images; p.24: Corbis; p.25: Bettmann–Corbis; p.26: Franklin D. Roosevelt Presidential Library & Museum; p.27: Time Life
Pictures–Getty Images; p.28: AP Photo; p.29 (top): Corbis; p.29 (bottom): The Granger Collection; p.30: AP Photo; p.31: Bettmann–Corbis; pp.
32–33: AP Photo; p.34: Time Life Pictures–Getty Images; p.35: Hulton Archive–Getty Images; p.36 (top): Franklin D. Roosevelt Presidential
Library & Museum; p.36 (bottom): Selwyn Tait–Corbis Sygma; p.37: Minnesota Historical Society–Corbis; p.38: Oscar White–Corbis; p.39: Time
Life Pictures–Getty Images; p.40 (top): Time Life Pictures–Getty Images; p.40 (bottom): Time Magazine Inc.; p.41 (top): The Granger Collection;
p.41 (bottom): Alex Wong–Getty Images; p.42: Seth Resnick–Corbis; p.43 (top): Swim Ink–Corbis; p.43 (bottom): Punchstock; p.44 (top):
royalty-free–Getty Images; p.44 (middle): The Granger Collection; p.44 (middle): Culver Pictures; p.44 (bottom): Hulton Archive–Getty Images;
back cover: Hulton Archive–Getty Images

Acknowledgments:
For TIME FOR KIDS: Editorial Director: Keith Garton; Editor: Jonathan Rosenbloom; Art Director: Rachel Smith; Designer: Jaye Medalia;
Photography Editor: Sandy Perez

 **Find out more at www.timeforkids.com/bio/froosevelt**

Franklin D. Roosevelt

▲ FRANKLIN D. ROOSEVELT was the first President to give regular radio broadcasts.

CHAPTER 1

The First Fireside Chat

Times were tough all across America. Millions of people were out of work, businesses and banks had closed, and too many people were hungry and homeless. In Houston, Texas, Myra King Whitson and her children crowded around the radio to hear the new President speak. It was around 9 P.M. on Sunday, March 12, 1933. At first the radio crackled and hissed. Then the President's voice was clear.

"The only thing we have to fear is fear itself."

—FRANKLIN D. ROOSEVELT

Franklin Delano Roosevelt talked about the country's money problems. He described his hopes and plans for the nation. To Whitson, he sounded calm and thoughtful. When she was done listening, Whitson wrote her new President a letter. "Our radio seemed to

▲ FAMILIES gathered around radio sets to listen to Roosevelt's fireside chats.

bring you to us in person," she wrote. "There is a deep happiness—a feeling that we have a real share in our government."

Every time he spoke on the radio, Americans listened closely. They wanted to hear the President talk about the country's problems and his ideas for fixing them. Roosevelt received thousands of letters after his first "fireside chat." Ordinary citizens—adults and children— wrote to Roosevelt with suggestions on how to help the nation overcome its problems.

During some of the saddest days in American history, President Roosevelt offered comfort with his hopeful words. He reminded people that they had the strength to carry on when things weren't going well. He encouraged them to keep trying.

Roosevelt had promised to find a job for every American who wanted to work. He also wanted to help people enjoy life. "Happiness lies not in the mere possession of money," he said. To Roosevelt, being happy meant enjoying nature, reading books, learning new things, and laughing with friends.

This is the story of Franklin Delano Roosevelt, a President who helped many Americans and who brightened some of the nation's darkest times.

▲ MILLIONS of Americans hoped Roosevelt would create jobs and improve their lives.

CHAPTER 2

Franklin's Early Years

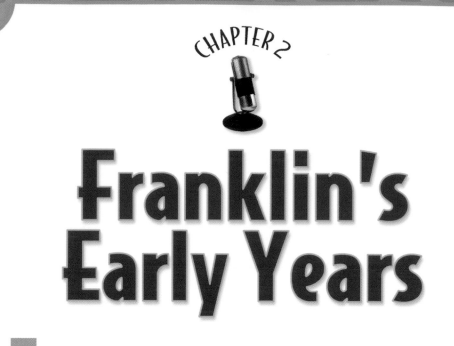

Franklin Delano Roosevelt was born on January 30, 1882. He was a big baby, with bright, blond hair. His mother, Sara, had many servants, but she loved Franklin so much that she fed, bathed, and dressed him herself every morning. He was her only child.

Sara was twenty-eight when Franklin was born. James, Franklin's father, was fifty-four. He was a businessman and spent much of his time taking care of the family's land

◀ SARA ROOSEVELT took excellent care of her only child.

4

▲ FRANKLIN spent a lot of time with his father, whom he called Popsy.

in Hyde Park, New York. The Roosevelts lived there in a huge home called Springwood, which overlooked the Hudson River. They also had a home in New York City, where they spent part of the year.

The Roosevelt family had been in America for a long time. Sara's ancestors had arrived at Plymouth Colony in Massachusetts in 1621. James's relatives had also been in America for generations. Franklin was born into a wealthy family with a proud history.

▲ FRANKLIN (far left) often played with his cousins—and a pet goat!

A Life of Luxury

Instead of going to elementary school, Franklin learned at home. Sara taught him how to read and write. Then, from age six on, Franklin studied with private tutors. They taught him Latin, German, and French. He also studied math, science, geography, and history. Franklin learned about America's past—its great leaders and its struggles. His tutors said he was smart and asked good questions.

Franklin worked hard, but he also had a lot of time for play. However, his parents didn't let him spend much time with children from the neighborhood. His overprotective mother worried he would learn bad habits from local kids. Instead, Franklin played alone or with his many cousins. He and his father were also close friends. James taught his son how to ice-skate, swim, and ride a horse. He also shared his love of nature with Franklin. The two often rode their horses or hiked through the woods and fields surrounding their home.

James encouraged his son to collect all kinds of things. Franklin started a stamp collection when he was ten years old. He gathered birds' nests and eggs, and wrote down everything he noticed about them in a notebook. Franklin also enjoyed taking photographs with a camera his parents gave him.

◄ HOP ON!
Franklin was about six when this photo was taken. He liked to ride around the grounds of his home.

Franklin had the chance to travel with his parents. James and Sara first took Franklin to Europe when he was just three years old. When he was nine, the Roosevelts spent a summer in Germany. From a very early age, Franklin saw how people lived all over the world. He got to meet lots of interesting people, listening carefully to what they had to say. And he experienced the differences between the United States and other countries. This knowledge proved to be useful when he was President.

While Franklin's education and travels were unusual for a boy his age, he was just like most kids in other ways. Sometimes he played tricks on people or got into mischief. Once, when he was nine, he hid in a tall tree while his parents searched everywhere for him. And at times he ran away from his teachers to avoid his reading or piano lessons. Luckily Franklin knew just the right thing to say to be forgiven every

time. Many years later, when he became President, he would use that charm to help win support from those who disagreed with him.

▼ SAY CHEESE! Franklin loved to take photographs.

A VISIT TO HYDE PARK

You can visit Springwood, the Roosevelt family home in Hyde Park, New York. Springwood is a National Historic Site open to visitors.

People can tour the home and see how the Roosevelt family lived. There are stables, an ice house (where food was kept cool), rose gardens, trails, and the grave site where Franklin and his wife, Eleanor, are buried. There is also the FDR Presidential Library and Museum, which has lots of exhibits about the President and his family.

Val-Kill, Eleanor's cottage, is just down the road.

For more information on Springwood and Val-Kill, go to the National Park Service website at www.nps.gov.

CHAPTER 3

Leaving Home for School

O nce Franklin turned fourteen, his parents sent him to boarding school. They chose Groton, a private school for boys in Massachusetts. When he arrived at Groton, Franklin was nervous about fitting in. Most of the other students had been at the school for two years and already knew one another. Franklin feared it would be hard to make friends.

Having studied with private tutors, Franklin was well prepared for school. He earned good grades, especially for neatness. And he was always

◀ THE GROTON CHAPEL was—and still is—a center of activity at the school.

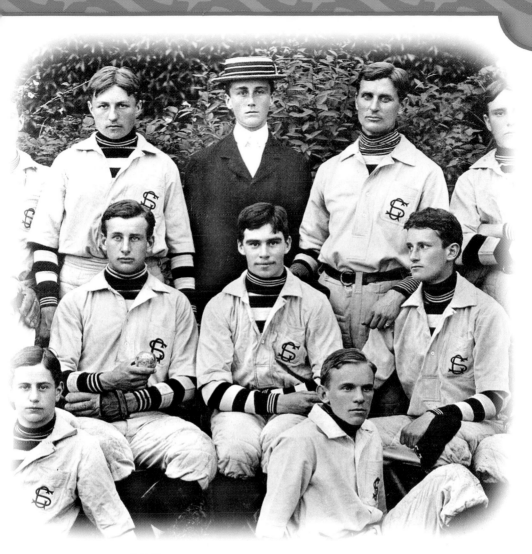

▲ **THE BOY IN THE HAT** is Franklin. He is surrounded by the baseball team at Groton.

on time for class. Sometimes the other boys thought Franklin was *too* well behaved. They teased him for being such a quiet student and for not being good at baseball or football. Franklin was good at tennis, sailing, and skating, but he had never played team sports. He was put on the worst baseball and football teams in the school.

◄ AS A YOUNG MAN, Franklin loved sailing and being on the water.

When Franklin was left off the good teams, he felt embarrassed. But he decided to find something he was good at. One day Franklin tried a Groton game called High Kick. Players would take turns jumping to kick a can hanging from the ceiling. Franklin found he could kick a can that was more than seven feet high! He was happy to win some respect at school.

While at Groton, Franklin became a skilled speaker and won many debates. With clever ideas and a strong voice, he convinced people with his words. Franklin said things he believed in and spoke from the heart.

Off to College

After graduating from Groton in 1900, Franklin went to Harvard University. His favorite subjects were history, government, and English.

But Franklin was not one of the best students in his class. Many of his professors gave him Cs. They said he should spend more time studying and less time partying.

However, one thing Franklin was very serious about was the school newspaper, *The Harvard Crimson*.

Franklin often spent whole afternoons and evenings at the paper's office. He wrote stories, edited other students' articles, and came up with new ideas for the college publication.

Franklin's friends on the staff thought he had great ways to improve the paper. They chose him as the editor during his final year. Franklin spent even more hours working on *The Harvard Crimson*. He also spent a lot of time thinking about his new love, a woman named Eleanor.

▲ FRANKLIN (in the bowtie) hung out with some college friends at his cousin's house.

CHAPTER 4

Going into Politics

Franklin first met Eleanor Roosevelt when they were children. They were fifth cousins and played together at family gatherings. When Franklin was in his last year at Harvard, they started going out together regularly. He visited her home in New York City. Eleanor showed him the homeless shelters where she volunteered. She also talked to him

▶ **ELEANOR** opened Franklin's eyes to people who were less fortunate than he.

▲ KIDS AS YOUNG AS TEN worked at dangerous factory jobs.

about the unfairness of young children working long hours in noisy, poorly lighted, and dangerous factories.

Franklin was impressed by the compassion Eleanor showed to everyone, including the poor. Her kindness rubbed off on Franklin, and he began to wonder what he could do to help others.

By Thanksgiving of 1903, Franklin told his mother he wanted to marry Eleanor. At first Sara was

▲ READING WAS A FAVORITE family activity for the Roosevelts.

disappointed. She thought her son was too young to
get married and that her son deserved a more beautiful
and stylish wife. But Sara gradually accepted her. After
all, Eleanor's uncle was President Theodore Roosevelt!

Franklin and Eleanor married on St. Patrick's Day
1905 in New York City. Franklin had just started
studying at Columbia University Law School. When he
finished school for the year, he and Eleanor went to
Europe for a long honeymoon. In May 1906 the
Roosevelts had their first child, Anna. Over the next
ten years, they had five more children—one of whom

died at an early age. Eleanor was a busy mother. She took care of a house full of children while Franklin was busy studying and working.

Meanwhile, Franklin finished law school and started a career as a New York City lawyer. But he found the work boring. Franklin dreamed of doing something different. Influenced by Eleanor, he wanted to do more for those who needed help.

Franklin Runs for the Senate

Franklin decided that he could do good for people by going into politics. To start his new career, in 1910, Roosevelt ran for the New York State Senate as a member of the Democratic Party. He gave ten speeches a day to voters in his Hyde Park district. Sometimes his voice would wear thin from talking so much.

At first Roosevelt was nervous about speaking to big crowds of strangers. But he soon

▶ FRANKLIN ENTERED POLITICS as a New York State Senator. He was an excellent speaker.

◄ EVEN IN 1920, when Franklin ran for vice president, political buttons were popular.

grew used to giving one speech after another. He remembered how easy it was at Groton to stand up and say what was on his mind. By the end of his campaign, Roosevelt was an excellent speaker. He criticized powerful, lazy politicians. He spoke about making New York's government work better, and the importance of preserving nature through conservation. He won the election, taking office for the first time.

Off to Washington

Roosevelt got sick with typhoid fever in 1912. Up for re-election to the New York State Senate, he didn't have the strength to campaign. But even though other people gave speeches for him, the young politician was so popular that he won easily.

Soon his thoughts turned to national politics. In 1913 he was chosen by President Woodrow Wilson to be the Assistant Secretary of the Navy in Washington, D.C. He made decisions about how the navy would prepare for the war that was about to break out—World War I.

Roosevelt did an outstanding job as naval secretary and earned the respect of other politicians. James M.

Cox, who was the Democratic Party's choice for President in 1920, asked Roosevelt to be his vice presidential running mate. The pair campaigned hard across the country but lost to Warren G. Harding and Calvin Coolidge.

About this time Franklin's relationship with Eleanor started to fade. The very busy couple weren't as close as they had been. Even though they were still married, they started to treat each other as friends and business partners rather than as husband and wife. But losing the election and struggling through marriage weren't Roosevelt's only problems.

▼ HATS OFF! James M. Cox and Franklin campaigned across the United States—but the pair lost the race.

CHAPTER 5

A Run for President

In 1921 Franklin came down with a virus that attacks the spinal cord. He was treated for polio, although some doctors today think he may have had a different illness. Soon he was paralyzed from the waist down.

Franklin worked hard to strengthen his body. He went to Warm Springs, Georgia, a place that some thought had healing waters. Franklin exercised and tried to build up his leg

◀ FRANKLIN spent time in Warm Springs, Georgia, where he relaxed, wrote, and swam.

▲ FRANKLIN'S DOG, FALA, and a neighbor were photographed with him. There are only a few photos of Franklin in a wheelchair.

muscles by swimming. But nothing seemed to help. He was a proud man and embarrassed that his illness kept him from walking on his own. Louis Howe, Franklin's close friend and advisor, and Eleanor helped him keep up his spirits. They encouraged him to keep fighting for the ideas he believed in. That inspired him to stay in politics.

However, his illness raised new questions. What would people think of a leader who couldn't walk on his own? Would they still vote for him? Franklin almost never allowed photos to be taken of him in his wheelchair or on crutches. He thought people might see them as a sign of weakness. Most Americans knew very little about Franklin's polio and wouldn't learn about it for years to come.

A New Job for Franklin

These difficult years didn't end Franklin's dreams of political greatness. He decided to run for governor of New York in 1928. Franklin was familiar with the state's problems and was still popular with New Yorkers. He won the election by 25,000 votes.

Even though Franklin suffered physical challenges, his spirit was as strong as ever. As governor of New

▼ FRANKLIN LIKED
to drive around New York
State and talk to citizens.

▲ **ELEANOR AND FRANKLIN** were surrounded by admirers on the campaign trail.

York, he pushed through several conservation bills and lowered taxes for farmers. After two years he was elected to another term. Then he was ready for an even bigger challenge. He decided to run for President of the United States.

Franklin knew that being President would not be an easy job. In 1929 the stock market had crashed. Businesses folded and jobs were hard to find. By 1932 twelve million Americans—about one in ten people—were out of work. Many banks had closed because

ROOSEVELT SAID IT!

"A nation that destroys its soils destroys itself. Forests are the lungs of our land, purifying the air and giving fresh strength to our people."

"A nation does not have to be cruel to be tough."

"If you treat people right they will treat you right . . . ninety percent of the time."

"Be sincere; be brief; be seated." (when giving a speech)

"There are many ways of going forward, but only one way of standing still."

"When you get to the end of your rope, tie a knot and hang on."

depositors had taken out their money. People didn't have enough to eat and worried about surviving. Many couldn't afford to pay their rent or buy medicine and winter clothing. Some were living in towns of cardboard shacks called Hoovervilles, named in anger after the current President, Herbert Hoover. The country was suffering from the Great Depression.

Franklin promised that if he became President, the government would offer more support to the poor, the homeless, and the jobless. He wanted to start up programs that would help people get back to work. In his speeches, he announced that he wanted to offer Americans a "New Deal."

▲ HOOVERVILLES, where homeless people lived, sprang up across the United States.

Some people worried that, because of his polio, Franklin wouldn't be strong enough to be President. But with Eleanor often at his side, he campaigned day after day across the country, proving he was healthy enough to be a leader. When Election Day finally arrived in November 1932, he won easily, carrying forty-two out of forty-eight states. At a celebration at Hyde Park, Franklin smiled and laughed, thanking his friends and family for helping him win. But the hardest job and the hardest times were still ahead.

"THE ONLY THING WE HAVE TO FEAR IS FEAR ITSELF--"

MARCH 4, 1933

▲ ROOSEVELT'S most famous quote decorates this photo from his inauguration.

CHAPTER 6

Welcome to the White House

On March 4, 1933, Franklin Delano Roosevelt, now often known as FDR, was sworn in as President. On that day he gave a famous speech. He said, "The only thing we have to fear is fear itself." He wanted to assure people that things would soon be better. His speech lifted people's spirits.

In his first hundred days as President, FDR started to improve life for all Americans with his New Deal program. One of the first things he did was to start to repair the bank system. He temporarily shut down all the banks and then allowed only the strongest banks—those with the most money

VOTE THE NEW DEAL

▲ FDR LISTENED to Americans' problems as he toured the country.

and best management—to reopen. He also got a law passed that insured the money people kept in banks. This helped to build more confidence in the system.

Next FDR began to create jobs for people. The first new program he started was the Civilian Conservation Corps (CCC). The Corps hired about 250,000 people to clean up national parks and forests. Although workers earned only about one dollar a day, they had an opportunity to support their families. Other new programs helped Americans find work rebuilding cities.

Slowly the new job programs put people back to work. But the improvements took time, and many people thought FDR wasn't acting fast enough. Others were alarmed that the government was spending so much money. But with his advisors helping him make decisions, FDR ignored critics and kept creating jobs. He refused to let people who didn't like his ideas stop him from trying to help the poorest Americans.

▲ **THIS EDITORIAL CARTOON** pokes fun at "alphabet" programs FDR started.

While her husband was busy being President, Eleanor was busy as First Lady. She traveled everywhere, visiting the poor and the sick. Eleanor wanted to make the country a safer, healthier place for everyone. She always reminded her husband about the importance of taking care of the nation's people.

On the Road to Recovery

When it came time for FDR to run for re-election in 1936, the United States was getting over some of its worst problems. The number of unemployed people had dropped. Farmers were earning more for their crops. Companies were making more money.

Some people still didn't like FDR's policies. In 1935 he had convinced Congress to raise the taxes of the wealthiest

◄ **REST EASY!** A woman shows off her Social Security card—the result of one of FDR's greatest programs.

Americans and companies. This helped pay for more job-creating programs and insurance plans for the poor. Many wealthy people didn't like paying more money to the government. But since most citizens supported the New Deal, FDR remained popular.

One of FDR's most important new programs was the Social Security System. It made sure that retired people would have an income after they stopped working. Social Security is still helping people today.

In the 1936 election, FDR won all but two states—Vermont and Maine. The President once again celebrated at his Hyde Park home after his victory.

MYSTERY PEOPLE

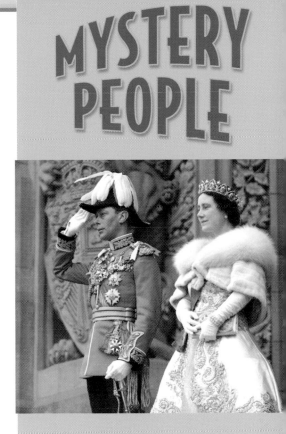

☞ **CLUE 1:** In 1939 this couple became the first British monarchs to ever visit the United States. FDR had invited them so that Britain and the United States would stay good friends.

☞ **CLUE 2:** The king and queen were served a picnic lunch of hot dogs at Hyde Park.

☞ **CLUE 3:** Their daughter is Queen Elizabeth II.

Who are they?

ANSWER: KING GEORGE VI AND QUEEN ELIZABETH

CHAPTER 7

America Goes to War

Soon after the 1936 election, FDR had a new set of problems. In Germany Adolf Hitler and his Nazi party were gaining power and threatening neighboring countries. Japan was moving against Korea and China. When Germany invaded Poland in 1939, many European and Asian nations went to war. World War II was under way.

▶ THE ATTACK ON PEARL HARBOR led to America's entry into World War II.

At first FDR said the United States would be better off staying out of the war. But then on December 7, 1941, Japan launched a surprise attack on Pearl Harbor, the American naval base in Hawaii. Almost 2,400 people were killed. Much of the Pacific fleet—twenty-one naval vessels—was sunk or damaged, and three hundred planes were destroyed. It was a painful day for the United States.

When the President was told of the attack, he knew the United States must fight back. The next day he spoke before Congress and asked the lawmakers to declare

▲ **THE PRESIDENT SIGNS** a Declaration of War as his aides look on.

war. The nation listened to FDR's speech on the radio as he announced that December 7 was "a date that would live in infamy." The American public agreed with the President, and Congress voted to go to war.

FDR, who had been elected for a record third time in 1940, met with Britain's Prime Minister, Winston Churchill, and the Soviet Premier, Joseph Stalin. They planned careful strategies for fighting the war. Roosevelt also worked with his advisors at home to find ways to attack Germany and Japan where they were weakest. Hundreds of thousands of soldiers from many countries died as fighting carried on.

Roosevelt was a strong, confident leader. In his fireside chats, he used his steady speaking voice to urge the country to be patient and proud—and to remain hopeful. The American people did all they could to help the war effort. They used less butter, sugar, and other goods so the U.S. could send them to soldiers overseas. Many women went to work because the men were fighting. The war created jobs and helped the economy as the nation did all it could to produce materials to win the fight.

▼ CHURCHILL, FDR, AND STALIN met several times during the war to plan strategies.

LIFE ON THE HOME FRONT

While soldiers were fighting overseas during World War II, Americans at home were being asked to sacrifice for the war effort. In 1942 the government gave each citizen (including kids) a book of ration coupons. These coupons were used to help buy scarce items such as sugar, butter, coffee, and beef. Homemakers had to put all their family's stamps together to plan meals. In addition, gasoline, rubber, and many metals were rationed so they could be used for war materials. People also recycled their metal and rubber scrap for the government.

During the war, Victory gardens sprang up across the

In 1944, as the war raged on in Europe and Asia, FDR decided to run again for President. He felt the nation needed his leadership despite the fact that he was in poor health. Again he won the election easily. Americans admired him and didn't want to change Presidents in wartime. During the inauguration ceremony marking the start of his fourth term, FDR's grandchildren joined him. This would be the last time the whole family would celebrate his victories.

country. The government encouraged people to grow fresh vegetables in their backyards, empty lots, and on school playgrounds as part of a food-growing plan. Soon six million Americans were raising vegetables.

◀ POSTERS reminded people to grow veggies.

WAR GARDENS FOR VICTORY
GROW VITAMINS AT YOUR KITCHEN DOOR

Many schools taught students how to plant vegetables so they could help out in the Victory gardens. And every morning kids said the Pledge of Allegiance as a sign

of patriotism. World maps hung in classrooms as teachers and students followed the war. Faraway places that were the scenes of huge battles, such as Iwojima and Guadalcanal in the Pacific, became familiar names.

The war brought Americans closer together to help their country. It was a time of sacrifice by soldiers in battle as well as by citizens at home.

◀ AMERICANS HAD RATION BOOKS for everything—from food to gasoline.

CHAPTER 8

A Sad Farewell

In 1945 FDR's health gradually got worse as his responsibilities got harder and harder because of the war. On April 12, 1945, he said to an assistant, "I have a terrific headache." Then he died suddenly in Warm Springs, Georgia. Vice President Harry S. Truman became the nation's thirty-third President.

A train carried FDR's body along the east coast to the funeral in Washington. Tens of thousands of people lined up to watch

◄ VICE PRESIDENT Harry S. Truman became President when FDR died.

▲ FDR'S FLAG-COVERED COFFIN traveled through the streets of Washington, D.C.

the train pass. Silently they honored their beloved leader. Thousands more people lined the streets of Washington, D.C., as FDR's casket was taken from Union Station.

A simple service took place in the White House. Diplomats from many countries came to pay their respects. Winston Churchill, Roosevelt's close friend and ally in the war, said that he felt he had "suffered a physical blow" and broke down in tears as he told the British people about the President's death. Through it all, Eleanor was calm. After the funeral Franklin was buried in the peaceful garden of his family home in Hyde Park.

A FINE FALA

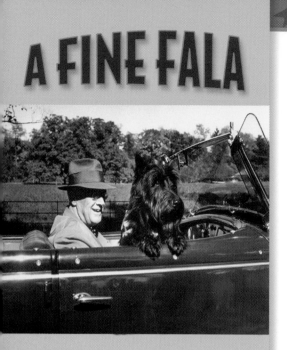

No presidential pet is more famous than Fala, Roosevelt's Scottish terrier.

Fala went everywhere with the President. The dog slept in a chair by Roosevelt's bed.

Fred D. Fair, a butler who worked for Roosevelt, remembers what life with Fala was like:

"Before the President's meal, I would fix Fala's food. But you couldn't serve Fala yourself. You handed it to the President, and he'd feed Fala out of his hand. Many times, I remember...important folks waiting for their supper until Mr. Roosevelt finished feeding Fala."

Fala is buried in Hyde Park a few yards from Franklin Roosevelt.

Americans mourned the death of a man who had been President for a history-making twelve years. He had led the nation through some of its darkest days of battle and its weakest moments of poverty.

In August 1945 the United States dropped two atomic bombs on Japan.

▼ **ROOSEVELT** appeared on eight covers of TIME magazine.

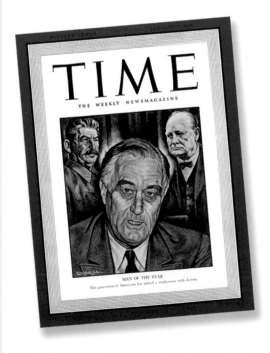

6c

FRANKLIN D. ROOSEVELT
U.S. POSTAGE

◄ A UNITED STATES postage stamp was designed and printed in FDR's memory.

More than two hundred thousand people were killed. The Japanese government surrendered, and World War II finally came to an end.

Roosevelt didn't get to see his country in victory. Yet his guidance, strong leadership, and confident words inspired others both at home and overseas. He had helped the country move toward prosperity and peace. Roosevelt's job programs gave millions of Americans dignity and pride. He turned a nation that was afraid into a nation that was hopeful and optimistic about the future. For that, he will always be remembered as one of the greatest American Presidents.

► THIS STATUE OF FDR in a wheelchair is at the Roosevelt Memorial in Washington, D.C.

Talking About Franklin

▲ Doris Kearns Goodwin

TIME reporter and author Jeremy Caplan spoke with Doris Kearns Goodwin about FDR. Goodwin, a historian, often writes about the U.S. Presidents.

Q. *How did FDR change the role of the President?*

A. He expanded the office, making it the center of action in a way it had not been for years. Citizens felt personally connected to him. His fireside chats were so popular that they drew audiences comparable to World Series or Superbowl games today.

Q. *What are FDR's greatest achievements?*

A. He led the American people through the two greatest crises in the twentieth century—the Great

◀ TODAY'S CLOSE TIES between Britain and the United States have their roots in Roosevelt's actions during World War II.

Depression and World War II. He and America's allies saved freedom and democracy.

Q. *Why did FDR care so much about the poor, having grown up wealthy?*

A. FDR had very little contact with poor people as a child. But the suffering he went through when polio left him paralyzed from the waist down gave him a great sympathy with others. Then, coming into office during the Great Depression, when so many millions were poor, he wanted to do all he could to help make things better. Also, Eleanor told him stories of average Americans, helping him understand their needs.

▶ RETIRED PEOPLE can enjoy their lives more, thanks to Social Security.

Franklin D. Roosevelt's
Key Dates

1882	Born on January 30, in Hyde Park, New York
1905	Marries his fifth cousin, Eleanor Roosevelt
1910	Wins seat in New York State Senate
1913	Named Assistant Secretary of the Navy
1921	Diagnosed with polio
1928	Elected governor of New York
1932	Elected President
1941	Asks Congress to declare war on Germany and Japan
1945	Dies on April 12, in Warm Springs, Georgia

1888 The ballpoint pen is invented.

1927 The first feature-length talking movie is made.

1936 The Spanish Civil War begins.

JOHN F. KENNEDY

About the Author of JOHN F. KENNEDY: Before moving to Delhi, India, where she is a freelance journalist, Ritu Upadhyay was an editor with TIME FOR KIDS®. Born and raised in Chicago, she has always been fascinated with the Kennedys and the legacy the family has created.

Photography and Illustration Credits:
Cover: JFK Collection—Zuma—Newscom; cover inset: Bettmann—Corbis; cover flap: AP Photo; title page: Time Life Pictures—Getty Images; contents page: Time Life Pictures—Getty Images; p. iv: AP Photo—John F. Kennedy National Historic Site; p.1: Library of Congress; p.2: Corbis; (photo corners): Photodisc; p.3: The John F. Kennedy Library; p.4: Corbis; p.5: The John F. Kennedy Library; p.6 (bottom left): Photodisc; p.6–7: The John F. Kennedy Library; p.7: Corbis; p.8: The John F. Kennedy Library; p.8 (bottom right): public domain; p.9: Culver Pictures; p.10 (top): The John F. Kennedy Library; p.10 (bottom left): Photodisc; p.11: The John F. Kennedy Library; p.12: The John F. Kennedy Library; p.13 (top): AP Photo; p.13 (bottom right): The John F. Kennedy Library; p.14: The John F. Kennedy Library; p.15: The John F. Kennedy Library; p.16: The John F. Kennedy Library; p.17 (bottom): public domain; p.17 (Fast Facts, top-bottom): Archive Photos—Newscom, Library of Congress, Chris Kleponis—Newscom, Time Life Pictures, Bettmann—Corbis; p.18: The John F. Kennedy Library; p.19: The John F. Kennedy Library; p.20: The John F. Kennedy Library; p.21: Hulton Archive—Getty Images; p.22: The John F. Kennedy Library; p.23: The John F. Kennedy Library; p.24: The John F. Kennedy Library; p.25 (bottom left): The John F. Kennedy Library; p.25 (inset): Bettmann—Corbis; p.26: Bettmann—Corbis; p.27: Bettmann—Corbis; p.28 (top): Smithsonian National Air and Space Museum; p.28 (bottom TV Frame): Photodisc; (photo): Time Life Pictures—Getty Images; p.29: The John F. Kennedy Library; p.30: Time Life Pictures—Getty Images; p.31 (top): The John F. Kennedy Library; p.31 (bottom left): Flip Schulke—Corbis; p.32: Time Life Pictures—Getty Images; p.33: Time Life Pictures—Getty Images; p.34: The John F. Kennedy Library; p.35: Hulton Archive—Getty Images; p.36: The John F. Kennedy Library; p.37 (top): Bettmann—Corbis; p.37 (bottom left): The John F. Kennedy Library; p.38 (top): Wally McNamee—Corbis; p.38 (bottom left): Bettmann—Corbis; p.39: AP Photo; p.40: JFK Collection—Zuma—Newscom; p.41 (top): Life Magazine—Time Inc.; p.41 (bottom right): Image Library; p.41 (bottom left): public domain; p.42: courtesy of Hugh Sidey; p.43 (top): AFP—Newscom; p.43 (bottom): Black Star; p.44 (top to bottom): Library of Congress; Corbis; AP Photo; Photoplay Archives/LGI; back cover: Library of Congress

Acknowledgments:
For TIME FOR KIDS: Editorial Director: Keith Garton; Editor: Jonathan Rosenbloom; Art Director: Rachel Smith; Photography Editor: Sandy Perez

 Find out more at <u>www.timeforkids.com/bio/kennedy</u>

JOHN F. KENNEDY

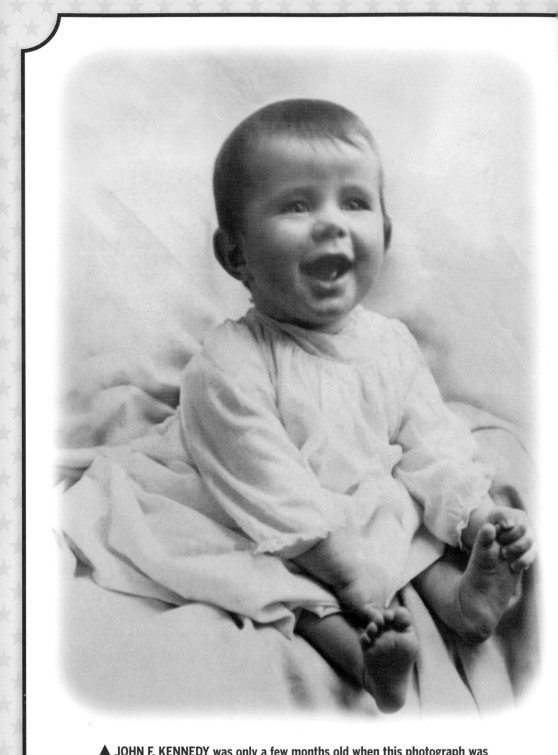

▲ JOHN F. KENNEDY was only a few months old when this photograph was taken. He was the second child of Joseph and Rose Kennedy.

JOHN F. KENNEDY

CHAPTER ONE

The Early
YEARS

On a cold spring day in Brookline, Massachusetts, a baby was born in the big frame house at 83 Beals Street. It was just a little after 3 P.M. on May 29, 1917, when John Fitzgerald Kennedy came into the world.

Jack, as his parents nicknamed him, was the second child of Joseph and Rose Kennedy. The baby was born into a rich and well-known family. His father was a successful businessman. His mother was the daughter of the mayor of Boston.

> **"Ask not what your country can do for you, but rather what you can do for your country."**
>
> JOHN F. KENNEDY

From the very beginning, little Jack was thin and sickly. When he was three, he almost died of an illness called scarlet fever. For a month his parents prayed by his bedside. He got better, but for the rest of his life he was always suffering from one sickness or another. His family used to tease him and say that if a mosquito were to bite Jack, the mosquito would die.

A Growing Family

Over the years, the Kennedy family grew to include nine children—four boys and five girls. The brood moved to a house with twelve rooms. Rose had to be very strict with her children so things wouldn't get out of control. Meals were served only at set times. If any children arrived late, they would not be able to have the food that had already been served. Rose also wanted the children to look neat and clean. Young freckle-faced Jack didn't like this. His thick hair tumbled messily across his

forehead. He hardly ever tucked in his shirt. His friend Lem Billings remembered that, as a kid, Jack was "usually tardy, forgetful, and often . . . sloppy."

Since Jack had so many brothers and sisters, his childhood was full of fun and activity. The Kennedys

▲ BABY JACK sits on a Massachusetts beach in 1918. The sea was always an important part of his life.

▲ **THE KENNEDYS SPENT SUMMERS** in Hyannis Port, where they swam and sailed. They also played against one another in sports such as touch football and tennis. Jack is the boy in the white shirt on the left.

spent their summers at a home in Hyannis Port, Massachusetts, a small town by the ocean. They learned to love the sea. Joseph wanted his children to do well at everything. "We want winners around here," he would say. That was a lesson the children would remember as they grew up.

There was a lot of friendly competition in the family. Jack used to get in many fistfights with Joe Jr., his older brother. Joe Jr. was bigger and stronger and could beat up Jack, who was small for his age. Outside the family, though, the Kennedy children were very loyal to one

another. Joe Jr. became Jack's coach and protector.

Jack didn't like being bossed around all the time, but secretly he admired his big brother.

At dinner the family would talk about politics and current events. Joe Jr. took part in mealtime debates with their father. From an early age he stood out as the young star in the family. He even said that one day he would become President. Jack, on the other hand, would rather play tricks than talk politics.

Good Old-Fashioned Values

Both parents often reminded the kids that the United States had been good to the Kennedys. Two of Jack's great-grandfathers sailed from Ireland to the United States in the 1800s to seek a better life. Rose said, "Whatever good things the family received from the country, you should return by performing some service for the country."

Even though Jack's father was very rich, he refused to spoil his children with large allowances. He wanted them to learn the value of money. When Jack was about eleven, he decided he needed more money. He wrote his father a letter titled, "A Plea for a Raise, by Jack Kennedy." He carefully explained how he was spending the forty cents a week he already earned. But, he said, as a Boy Scout, he needed more money to buy supplies. "I have to buy canteens, blankets, search-lights—things that will last me for years," he wrote. Jack's father agreed to the raise after reading his son's convincing letter. Jack proved he could write well and could persuade people with his words. That would serve him well for the rest of his life.

▶ COPS AND ROBBERS
Jack used to dress up as a police officer. He was always getting into mischief and playing good-natured tricks on people.

The Making of a
LEADER

When Jack was ten, he was sent away to Choate, a private school in Connecticut. He lived there and came home for holidays. Jack had developed a love of reading during all those days spent sick in bed as a young child. But in school he got only average grades. He was always thought of as the little brother of Joe Jr., who made better grades and was better at sports. Jack often was in trouble for not listening to his teachers. But he was gifted at making friends. It was hard to resist his cheerful personality. One of his

▶ FOOTBALL was an important family sport. Jack is about ten years old in this picture. The "D" stands for Dexter School, where he went before Choate.

former teachers remembered, "When he flashed his smile, he could charm a bird off a tree."

After Choate he decided to go to Harvard University in Cambridge, Massachusetts, like his father and brother. Jack was popular at the school, but he still didn't get very good grades.

In 1938, during Jack's third year of college, President Franklin D. Roosevelt named Joseph Kennedy Sr. the American ambassador to Great Britain. (An ambassador is a representative in a foreign country.) Jack went to England to visit his father. He traveled to many countries in Europe. He met lots of people and listened to their opinions about current events. When he returned to Harvard, he wrote a paper about why England did not stand up to the German dictator, Adolph Hitler. His paper became a best-selling book, *Why England Slept,* in 1940.

Jack wasn't sure what to do after he graduated from Harvard. He had studied American government, but he didn't want to go to law school. He decided to join the U.S. Navy in 1941. Three months later, the Japanese bombed Pearl Harbor, Hawaii—the headquarters of the Pacific fleet. When that happened, the United States entered World War II. Jack rose to the rank of commander in the navy.

WHY ENGLAND SLEPT

JOHN F. KENNEDY

▲ ON DECEMBER 7, 1941, Japanese planes bombed Pearl Harbor, Hawaii, in a surprise attack. The next day the United States entered World War II.

Jack Becomes a Hero

On August 2, 1943, Jack faced the biggest challenge of his life. The patrol boat Jack was in charge of got separated from the other American forces in the Pacific Ocean. At 2:30 A.M. a Japanese ship suddenly plowed through the small boat and cut it in half. Two of Jack's crew died. Three were badly hurt. The survivors floated in the water, holding on to a piece of the boat all night. Jack decided their only chance to live was to swim to a nearby small island. One man was too injured and weak to move. Jack clenched the straps of

▲ SETTING SAIL on PT 109, the small ship Jack commanded

the man's lifejacket between his teeth and towed him to safety. He swam like that for five hours, until they reached the shore of the island. Days later the crew was rescued. Jack returned to the United States and was given two important medals for his courage and leadership. One was the Navy and Marine Corps Medal. The other was the Purple Heart Medal. The Kennedys were proud of their son and brother, and they were very grateful that he returned from the war alive.

Dad's Big Dream

In the spring of 1944, the Kennedy family received terrible news. Joe Jr., who was serving in the air force, was killed while flying on a dangerous mission. Joe Sr. was very upset by the death. He had had big dreams for his eldest son. As time passed, Joe Sr. convinced Jack that now it was his duty to go into politics. His father told him he wanted Jack to be the country's first Roman Catholic President. Some people thought a Roman Catholic could never be elected President of the United States. Years later these people would be proved wrong.

▶ ANCHORS AWEIGH!
Jack Kennedy poses proudly in his navy uniform. He served as a commander.

Entering
POLITICS

J ack rose to his father's challenge. In 1946 he ran for the United States House of Representatives from his home state of Massachusetts. The entire family helped with the campaign. His father asked his powerful and wealthy friends for support. Jack's mother gave tea parties for women in the community. Jack and his

MORE JOBS • MORE HOUSING • MORE INDUSTRY

JOHN F. **KENNEDY**

For CONGRESS • 11TH DISTRICT • PRIMARIES TUES. JUNE 18

◀ RUNNING FOR CONGRESS was John Kennedy's first try at public office. The issues that were important to him are written on the banner behind him. He won!

▲ JACK liked nothing better than going out and meeting people in their hometowns. It gave him a good idea of what issues were important to them.

brothers and sisters knocked on doors asking for people's votes. The hard work, and the famous Kennedy name, paid off. Jack won the election in November.

In Washington twenty-nine-year-old Congressman Kennedy stood out as a young, handsome politician. But as always, he was in bad health. Doctors decided he had

▶ BACK PAIN didn't stop Kennedy from giving speeches while running for office.

Addison's disease, an illness that destroys part of the adrenal glands. Addison's disease made Kennedy too weak to fight off other sicknesses. The Kennedy family kept the disease a secret. They feared it would put an end to Jack's political career. Kennedy also had serious back pain but was able to deal with it by taking many kinds of medicine.

Jack and Jackie Get Married

In 1952 Kennedy ran for the United States Senate and won. At the same time he was dating a beautiful young newspaper photographer. Her name was Jacqueline Bouvier. Like Kennedy she came from a wealthy family. She was intelligent, graceful, and stylish. The handsome senator asked Jackie to be his wife. Their marriage on September 12, 1953, was one of the most talked about events of the year.

In 1954 Kennedy had to have a serious back operation. During the months he spent in the hospital recovering, he wrote a book, *Profiles in Courage*. It described

▲ SIGN HERE!
People often asked Kennedy to autograph his book.

▲ JACK AND JACKIE's wedding reception took place at Jackie's family home in Rhode Island. The wedding was reported in many magazines and newspapers.

the bravery of a few politicians who fought for their ideals to make the United States a better place in which to live. Kennedy later won the Pulitzer Prize in biography, one of the nation's top writing prizes. The senator proved he was a charming politician *and* an intelligent writer.

The Race For
PRESIDENT

After getting experience in Congress, Kennedy, with the urging of his family, decided it was time to run for President. In July 1960 he won the Democratic Party's nomination for the race. With the help of his younger brother Robert, Kennedy ran a strong campaign. He promised a "new frontier" for Americans. Kennedy and his running mate, Lyndon Baines Johnson of Texas, ran

▲ CAMPAIGNING in New Hampshire, Kennedy tried to get people to vote for him.

against Richard Nixon, the Republican Party's choice. Nixon was much older and more experienced than Kennedy. He was serving as the Vice President of the United States under Dwight D. Eisenhower. But Kennedy used his youth to his advantage. The first ever presidential debates on television were held during the 1960 election. On television Kennedy looked handsome and smart. He spoke well and

▲ PEOPLE who wanted Kennedy to win the election wore this button.

had a lot of energy. Richard Nixon came off as tired, old, and unprepared.

It was a very close race, but Kennedy won. At the age of forty-three, John Fitzgerald Kennedy became the thirty-fifth President of the United States. He was the youngest man ever elected to the highest office in the land.

Kennedy came to Washington, D.C., with new and exciting ideas. One of his greatest ideas was starting the Peace Corps. He urged Americans to volunteer to work in countries around the world. The volunteers served as teachers to help people in poorer nations improve their lives. Peace Corps workers taught people to read and write. They taught better ways to farm, and how to lead healthier lives.

More than forty years after the Peace Corps began, volunteers today are still helping others who are less fortunate.

THE 35TH
U.S. PRESIDENT

Kennedy was sworn in as President of the United States on January 20, 1961. It was a very cold day, and eight inches of snow covered the capital! But Kennedy managed to warm the hearts of most of the people who watched him. His famous inauguration speech was one of the most memorable of all time. Kennedy challenged Americans to "ask not what your country can do for you, but rather what you can do for your country." His speech inspired Americans to be active citizens and to make the United States and the world a better place.

▲ HIDE-AND-SEEK was a favorite game of John Jr. One of his favorite places to hide was under his dad's desk in the Oval Office, where the President worked.

Life at the White
HOUSE

The Kennedys brought a new spirit and excitement to the capital. Americans were excited to see a young family in the White House. The Kennedys had two children. Their daughter, Caroline, was just three years old when her father became President. Their son, John Jr., was only two months old. They were the first young children to live in the White House since the early 1900s.

Jackie added a preschool and kindergarten to the third floor

CAROLINE gives baby John a kiss after they moved to the White House. ▲

▲ IMPORTANT VISITORS
The President claps as John Jr. and Caroline skip around the Oval Office.

of the White House. There was also a new swimming pool and a giant tree house. Even though he had a busy schedule, President Kennedy always took time out of his day to play with his children. Caroline rode her pet pony, Macaroni, on the White House lawn. John Jr. loved to play under the President's desk. Once he hid

there during a meeting his father was having with an important British leader. As the talks grew tense, little John jumped out from under the desk and screamed, "I'm a big bear and I'm hungry!" The President and his guest laughed. Kennedy told his visitor, "You may think this is strange behavior in the office of the President of the United States, but in addition to being the President, I also happen to be a father."

A Famous First Lady

The President and First Lady hosted many beautiful parties at the White House. They enjoyed music and invited different artists to perform at official dinners. Jackie Kennedy had a big influence on fashion. Women copied her style, from her clothes to the way she wore her hair.

People around the world were equally charmed

▲ COMMAND PERFORMANCE
The Kennedys entertained world leaders at the White House. After dinner they would often have a musician play. Here they are speaking with Pablo Casals, a famous cellist.

with the First Family. When the President visited world leaders, people were awestruck by the beautiful First Lady and the handsome and funny President. Thousands of French people poured into the streets to get a look at the couple during their trip to Paris in 1961. Jackie's every move was followed as if she were a movie star. At a news conference in Paris, the

President started a speech by saying jokingly, "I am the man who accompanied Jacqueline Kennedy to Paris."

President Kennedy and his family quickly became the closest thing the United States had to royalty. The White House was called Camelot during those years. It meant a time of fairy-tale splendor, hope, and great happiness.

▲ PARTY!
The Kennedys get ready for a state dinner. The man behind Jackie is Vice President Lyndon Johnson.

THE WHITE HOUSE TOUR

Jackie Kennedy was proud of the White House and wanted the inside to be as beautiful as the outside. She convinced people to donate the best American furniture, antiques, and artworks to the President's home.

In 1962 Jackie showed off the redecorated White House on television. For the first time, Americans could visit the President's home without leaving their living rooms. About eighty million people tuned in to watch this special broadcast.

Trouble Around the

WORLD

From the moment he became President, Kennedy was very focused on international problems. The United States and the Soviet Union were bitter rivals. The Soviet Union had a communist form of government, and the U.S. was a democracy. (In a communist country, people cannot vote for their leaders or own property like they can in a democracy.) The rivalry between the Soviet Union and the U.S. was called

Dr. FIDEL CASTRO

◀ **FIDEL CASTRO** first came to power in Cuba in 1959. To get away from his rule, many Cubans came to the United States to live.

the Cold War. No
battles were
actually fought
between the two
powers, but both
countries tried to
have more
influence over the
world. This led to
serious military
problems.

In 1961
Kennedy sent
American troops
to Cuba, a nation ninety miles off the coast of Florida.
He wanted to overthrow Fidel Castro, the country's
communist leader. Castro was supported by the Soviet
Union. In the Bay of Pigs invasion, the U.S. helped a
large group of Cubans try to get rid of Castro. But that
did not happen. The President was upset. This was a
big failure for him.

▶ MISSILES IN CUBA caused big problems for the United States. Here, Kennedy meets with some pilots who took photos of the missiles.

Cuba's Missiles

Less than a year later, the United States learned that the Soviet Union had sent dangerous nuclear weapons to Cuba. Some of the weapons were aimed at the United States. For days the world thought the United States and the Soviet Union might go to war. But Kennedy ended the crisis through talks with Soviet leader Nikita Khrushchev.

Another troubled place was Berlin. In 1947 this East German city had been split in two: communist-controlled East Berlin and free, democratic West Berlin. In 1961 the Soviets began to build a concrete wall topped with sharp wire between the two sections of the city. They wanted to stop people from leaving East Berlin for West Berlin. The Berlin Wall became a symbol of

▲ EAST MET WEST when Kennedy met with the head of the Soviet Union, Nikita Khrushchev. They talked about the problems between their nations.

the struggle between communism and democracy. In June 1963 Kennedy went to Berlin. He promised that democracy would win out and the two sides of the city would be united someday. And he was right. Twenty-six years later, the wall was torn down. East and West Berlin were joined together again.

▼ A COUNTRY DIVIDED
President Kennedy visited Berlin, Germany, in 1963. He visited the Berlin Wall, which divided the city in two.

The Country Moves
AHEAD

There were problems around the world and problems at home as well. A young African American leader named Martin Luther King Jr. was leading a peaceful and fast-growing civil rights movement in the South. Blacks were tired of being treated like second-class citizens. They wanted to be

LINCOLN'S

On January 1, 1863, President Abraham Lincoln issued an Emancipation Proclamation. This statement set slaves in the South free. The proclamation did not totally end slavery in America, but it was a big step toward giving blacks basic freedoms. Many people criticized Lincoln because he freed only slaves who lived in

▲ **ABRAHAM LINCOLN was one of Kennedy's heroes.**

▲ KENNEDY fought for equal rights for African Americans. He often met with civil rights leaders about making peaceful changes. Martin Luther King Jr. is third from the left.

equal with white people. Segregation (keeping blacks and whites apart) was against the law in the United States. But it still took place in many southern states.

EMANCIPATION PROCLAMATION

southern states. But it did lead to the Thirteenth Amendment to the Constitution, which outlawed slavery in the United States in 1865. Despite winning freedom, blacks still had a long road ahead toward equality and civil rights.

▲ MARCH ON WASHINGTON
In August 1963, more than 250,000 people marched for civil rights.

MYSTERY PERSON

☞CLUE 1: I am often called the "Mother of the Civil Rights Movement."

☞CLUE 2: On my way home from work on December 1, 1955, I was arrested in Montgomery, Alabama, for refusing to give up my bus seat to a white passenger.

☞CLUE 3: My arrest led blacks to stop using the bus system. They demanded that buses no longer be separated into different sections for whites and blacks. The bus boycott started the push for equal rights for blacks all over the South.

Who am I?

ANSWER: ROSA PARKS

In some places African Americans were refused jobs because of their skin color. They were not allowed to go to the same schools or restaurants as white people. They had to sit in the back of the bus or give up their seats to white people. African Americans couldn't drink from the same water fountain or use the same bathroom as whites. They couldn't stay in the same hotels. They had to use separate waiting rooms in bus stations. Some people made it hard for blacks to vote in elections.

Protesters decided to do something about these problems. In many southern cities, African Americans refused to ride city buses. They began

protests and strikes to tell the world about the unfairness. This was often met by anger on the part of some white people. Many African Americans were yelled at or beaten for trying to get equal rights.

Kennedy was very angry that black people had fewer opportunities, based on the color of their skin. He decided strong U.S. government action needed to be taken. "One hundred years of delay have passed since President Lincoln freed the slaves, yet their heirs, their grandsons are not fully free," he said. In 1963 President Kennedy proposed a civil rights bill that was later passed by the United States Congress.

The bill called for strong laws to protect the rights of African Americans and to make sure blacks and whites could go to the same schools.

The Race for Space

After sending the first human into orbit, the Soviet Union was ahead of the United States in exploring space. President Kennedy wanted the U.S. to lead in space exploration. In 1961 he asked Congress for money to help build rockets.

He said, "I believe this nation should commit itself to achieving the goal, before this decade is out, of landing a man on the moon and returning him safely to the Earth."

Just a few years earlier, Kennedy's bold idea might have seemed impossible. But within one year of his speech to Congress, John Glenn became the first American to orbit the Earth. And in 1969 two American astronauts became the first people to walk on the moon—and return safely to Earth.

Kennedy's dream had come true. Space was finally being explored!

◄ THE APOLLO 11 CREW pose proudly in their spacesuits. Michael Collins (center) piloted the spacecraft, while Neil Armstrong (left) and Edwin "Buzz" Aldrin (right) walked on the moon.

CHAPTER EIGHT

A Tragic
TRIP

November 22, 1963, was a clear, sunny day in Dallas, Texas. President Kennedy and the First Lady traveled to the city on a speaking tour. Many people in Texas did not agree with the President's policies on civil rights and other issues. Kennedy hoped to gain support by traveling there.

Tens of thousands of people came out to greet the President. They cheered, clapped, and carried welcome signs. Kennedy sat in the back

▲ ARRIVAL IN DALLAS
The Kennedys leave Air Force One—the President's personal plane.

of a black convertible with Jackie and waved to the crowds. Suddenly gunshots pierced through the cheering crowds. President Kennedy had been shot twice! He was rushed to a hospital, but doctors could not save him. John Fitzgerald Kennedy died at the age of forty-six.

◀ **VICE PRESIDENT LYNDON JOHNSON** is sworn in as President on board Air Force One. His wife, Lady Bird, is on the left. Mrs. Kennedy is on the right.

The President's suspected killer, Lee Harvey Oswald, was caught and arrested immediately. Oswald was later shot and killed by another man. (To this day some people believe that Oswald did not act alone in the shooting. But that has never been proven.)

Vice President Lyndon Johnson, his wife, and Jackie Kennedy were taken back to Air Force One. On board the

▲ JOHN KENNEDY JR. salutes his father's coffin at the funeral. This famous photograph touched the hearts of many Americans.

plane, Johnson was sworn in as the thirty-sixth President of the United States.

The entire world mourned the loss of the beloved young President Kennedy. In shock and grief, leaders from many nations came to the funeral.

Hundreds of thousands of people lined the streets of Washington, D.C., to pay their respects as the President's coffin slowly wound its way through the capital. Millions more watched on television as the nation came to a full

JOHN, JACKIE, & CAROLINE

AFTER THE WHITE HOUSE

Eleven days after the President's death, Jackie, Caroline, and John Jr. moved out of the White House. Jackie wanted her kids to succeed in whatever they decided to do. "Just remember how proud your father was and would have been, and never forget that," she told them. Jackie went on to have a successful career as a book editor. She died in 1994 at the age of sixty-five. John Jr. went to law school and started a magazine. He died in a plane crash in 1999. Caroline is married with three children. She is a lawyer and author who works hard to keep alive the special memories of her family.

▲ JOHN KENNEDY was often happiest and most relaxed when he was sailing. He loved the sea.

stop in memory of the President. A riderless black horse slowly walked behind the coffin. It was a symbol of a fallen leader.

The First Lady walked behind the coffin for more

▶ **THE PRESIDENT** was remembered on this cover of LIFE magazine, on U.S. half dollars, and on postage stamps.

LIFE

PRESIDENT
JOHN F.
KENNEDY
—
1917
1963

NOVEMBER 29 · 1963 · 25¢

than a mile. Jackie stayed strong through the terrible tragedy. Her strength and grace during that terrible time brought comfort to the entire country.

Kennedy Remembered

John Fitzgerald Kennedy was President of the United States for just over one thousand days. During that time, he made a strong impression on the nation and the world. President Kennedy will always be remembered for his ability to get people to do their best and to meet challenges. He wanted all Americans to take an active role in helping others, especially those who are less fortunate.

Shortly before his death Kennedy said, "A man may die, nations may rise and fall, but an idea lives on."

Talking About
KENNEDY

▲ Hugh Sidey

TIME FOR KIDS editor Dina El Nabli and Kid Reporter Daniel Bonner spoke with Hugh Sidey, a reporter who knew John F. Kennedy and wrote a book about his presidency. Here's what Sidey had to say.

Q: *What is your fondest memory of President Kennedy?*

A: Once I went to interview him, and he said, "Let's take a swim." That's the only underwater interview I've ever had.

Q: *What did the Kennedys bring to the White House that was unique?*

A: The Kennedys realized that part of the American dream was the search for beauty in everyday doings.

► THE SPACE SHUTTLE *ATLANTIS* takes off. Many people say it's because of John F. Kennedy that we have explored space.

Q: *What do you think JFK would be fighting for today?*

A: To save the environment, limit nuclear arms, and make sure that everybody has equal opportunities.

Q: *Is there a program, like the Peace Corps, that President Kennedy would support today?*

A: Kennedy might have been very interested in a national service program of some kind. Every young person would have to sign up as a volunteer and serve in some way at home or abroad. He believed people should do good for others.

◄ AMERICANS join the Peace Corps in order to help others. The Corps, started by Kennedy, is still going strong.

JOHN F. KENNEDY'S
KEY DATES

1917 Born on May 29, in Brookline, Massachusetts

1920 Women get the right to vote in the United States.

1940 Graduates from Harvard; publishes *Why England Slept*

1943 Leads navy ship crew to safety

1946 Elected to United States Congress

1952 Elected to United States Senate

1953 Marries Jacqueline Bouvier

1950 Korean War begins.

1957 Wins Pulitzer Prize for *Profiles in Courage*

1961 Inaugurated as President

1962 Cuban missile crisis

1955 Elvis Presley becomes the first rock star.

1963 Proposes civil rights bill; assassinated on November 22, in Dallas, Texas

MR. PRESIDENT HOW LONG MUST WOMEN WAIT FOR LIBERTY

Ronald Reagan

About the Author of RONALD REAGAN: "Reading has always been as great a passion for me as writing is," says Denise Lewis Patrick, a native of Natchitoches, Louisiana. Author of more than twenty-five books for young people, she lives in New Jersey with her husband and their four sons.

Photography and Illustration Credits:
Cover: Michael Evans–ZUMA Press; cover inset: royalty free–Getty Images; cover flap: Ronald Reagan Presidential Library; title page: Everett Collection; contents page: Time Life Pictures–Getty Images; p.iv: AP Photo; p.1: Time Life Pictures; p.2: AP Photo–Ron Edmonds; p.3: AP Photo; p.4: Time Life Pictures; p.5: AP Photo; p.6: AP Photo; pp.6–7: AP Photo; p.8: Ronald Reagan Presidential Library; p.9: AP Photo; p.10: Ronald Reagan Presidential Library; p.11: Ronald Reagan Presidential Library; p.12: Ronald Reagan Presidential Library; p.13: AP Photo; p.14: AP Photo; p.15: Photodisc; p.16: Lou Valentino Collection; p.17: AP Photo; p.18: Ronald Reagan Presidential Library; p.19: courtesy Universal International Pictures; p.20: AP Photo; p.21: Ken James–Corbis; p.22: AP Photo; p.23: Bob Rowan–Corbis; p.24: Bettmann–Corbis; p.25: AP Photo; p.26: Ronald Reagan Presidential Library; p.27: Bettmann–Corbis; p.28: Ronald Reagan Presidential Library; p.29: Ronald Reagan Presidential Library; p.30 (top): Ronald Reagan Presidential Library; p.30 (bottom): Ronald Reagan Presidential Library; p.31: Ronald Reagan Presidential Library; p.32: Bettman–Corbis; p.33: Ronald Reagan Presidential Library; p.34: Ronald Reagan Presidential Library; p.35: Ronald Reagan Presidential Library; p.36: royalty free–Getty Images; p.37: Ronald Reagan Presidential Library; p.38: AP Photo–Ron Edmonds; p.39: Ronald Reagan Presidential Library; p.40: AP Photo–Joe Cavaretta; pp.40–41: AP Photo–Stephan Savoia; p.41: Michael Evans–Corbis; p.42: Rich Frishman; p.43 (top): Ron Chapple–Getty Images; p.43 (bottom): Reuters–Corbis; p.44 (top): Everett Collection; p.44 (middle): AP Photo–Ford Motor Company; p.44 (middle): AP Photo–Neil Armstrong/NASA; p.44 (bottom): AP Photo–Eric Risberg; back cover: Time Life Pictures–Getty Images

Acknowledgments:
For TIME FOR KIDS: Editorial Director: Keith Garton; Editor: Jonathan Rosenbloom; Art Director: Rachel Smith; Designer: Michele Weisman; Photography Editor: Sandy Perez

 Find out more at www.timeforkids.com/bio/reagan

Ronald Reagan

> *"There are no great limits to growth because there are no limits of human intelligence, imagination, and wonder."*
>
> —RONALD REAGAN

▲ THOUSANDS OF PEOPLE watched Ronald Reagan being sworn in as President on January 20, 1981. Ronald's wife, Nancy, was front and center for the ceremony.

Chapter 1

Any Child in America

The winter day was icy cold, and the skies over Washington, D.C., surely were going to fill with snow. The weather had been so much warmer and sunnier at the California ranch Ronald and Nancy Reagan left behind!

But the Reagans were excited as their dark limousine pulled up to the beautiful White House. On that day, January 20, 1981, Ronald Wilson Reagan had just been sworn in as the fortieth President of the United States.

The new President held hands with his wife as they passed through the famous rooms. There

▲ *TIME* MAGAZINE featured Reagan on its 1980 cover. It was issued just after he was elected President.

▲ **A SNOW-COVERED** lawn welcomed the Reagans to the White House.

was the elegant East Room, where large parties and dinners were held. Then came the Oval Office, where other Presidents had worked before him. At last he and Nancy entered the family rooms. This is where the Reagans would live for at least the next four years.

As a boy Reagan had once lived in an apartment over the store where his father worked. There wasn't a lot of extra spending money when he was growing up.

Like many kids, he dreamed about being wealthy, successful, and famous. Finally his dreams had come true.

President Reagan later said, "If I could do this, then truly any child in America had an opportunity to do it."

He had been an athlete, a radio announcer, a movie actor, a union leader, and a state governor. Now he was seventy years old—the oldest person ever elected President. When many people were retiring, Reagan was beginning the most important job of his life. Could he lead a nation?

Ronald Reagan had been elected at a time when many Americans were struggling because they had lost jobs. Many thought the United States was less powerful than it had been. Reagan believed Americans had forgotten their dreams— for themselves and their nation. He was ready to help his country remember how to dream.

▲ RONALD WAS BORN in this apartment above a store in Tampico, Illinois.

Young Dutch Grows Up

Jack Reagan smiled when his son Ronald was born at home on February 6, 1911. "He looks like a fat little Dutchman," he said. "But who knows, he might grow up to be President someday!"

Ronald's mother, Nelle, was happy that their son was healthy. But when two-year-old Neil saw his baby brother, he was disappointed. He'd wanted a sister!

◄ BABY RONNIE was a few months old when this picture was taken.

Although Dutch was born in Tampico, Illinois, the Reagan family moved many times when the boys were young. Jack sold shoes, but he was fired from jobs because he had a problem with drinking too much. Nelle explained to the boys that their father had a sickness, and that he was trying to get better. Jack never quite recovered from his alcoholism. Over the years the family had some hard times because of that. Yet Ronald still remembered his father as charming, easygoing, and a wonderful storyteller.

Nelle stayed at home, taking care of the children. Sometimes she sewed clothes or worked with Jack to make extra money. She was very religious and expected her sons to pray and to attend church. Nelle also told them to believe in their dreams.

Hello, Dixon

The Reagans finally settled in Dixon, Illinois, in 1920. Going to so many different schools hadn't been easy for the Reagan boys. At first shy Dutch didn't make new friends as quickly as his more outgoing brother did. Neil, who was called Moon by the family, was a better athlete.

▲ **HOME, SWEET HOME!**
In 1920 the Reagans moved to this neat house in Dixon, Illinois.

Dutch spent a lot of time reading—including a book about wolves that he especially loved—but he still enjoyed sports very much. He played his first football game with Moon and some friends when he was nine years old. Although he wasn't very good at the sport, he was hooked. He also ice-skated and swam. Soon skinny little Dutch became an excellent swimmer.

Besides playing sports, Dutch and Moon had fun in other ways. Sometimes, when the boys had a few nickels, they would go to the movies. On many evenings Nelle would make popcorn and read the boys stories. She loved poems and plays, and she performed at schools and churches in nearby towns. Nelle tried to get her sons to join her. When Dutch was about ten, he memorized a speech and then recited it during a show. The audience applauded. He didn't know it yet, but that stage experience would play an important part in his life.

Dutch had another memorable experience, which got him into trouble. One July Fourth, when he was eleven, he bought some illegal fireworks and set them off near the town's bridge. A police officer took him to the station, where his father paid the $14.50 fine. Dutch had to work hard to pay back his father.

◀ **DUTCH LIKED TO PLAY** football. He is second from the left in this picture. Check out the uniforms!

Dutch the Teenager

When Dutch and Moon became teenagers, they looked for summer jobs to help out their family. They did odd jobs for the Ringling Brothers Circus. Dutch also worked on a building construction crew. The hard work carrying bricks made him strong. His body filled out, and he had muscles!

When Dutch was fifteen, he got a job as a lifeguard at Lowell Park Beach. Dutch was popular there. Everyone at the beach could pick him out from the crowd, with his broad shoulders and shiny dark hair. Dutch worked seven days a week, twelve hours a day. He was an excellent lifeguard and worked hard at this important job. During seven summers there, he rescued seventy-seven people.

At Dixon High School he made

◄ DUTCH was a hard-working and popular teenager.

good grades but only won a spot on the second-string football team. Dutch was disappointed, since he loved the sport. He was stubborn, though, and he didn't give up. His determination got him a spot as right guard on the first team for his senior year.

He also discovered something new in high school—acting. Margaret Cleaver, a girl Dutch liked, was in the drama club at Dixon High. Dutch joined, too. Dutch also knew Margaret was planning to go to college after she graduated. Not many people from Dixon went to college. No one in Dutch's family had gone.

Nelle encouraged both her sons to apply to college. Moon wasn't interested, but Dutch was. He figured he could play football there, and he could see Margaret all the time. He only had to figure out how to earn the money he needed to pay for his education.

Chapter 3

Dutch Goes to College

After Dutch graduated from high school in 1928, he went to Eureka College—the same school Margaret was attending—in the tiny town of Eureka, Illinois. Dutch talked to a few people at the college and got a football scholarship that covered his school fees. To pay for his books and his room, he got a job as a waiter in the school dining room.

Dutch was not as good at football as many of his

◄ **DUTCH WARMS UP** before a college football game.

teammates. But he *was* good at acting. When Dutch wasn't playing ball, he took part in the drama group with Margaret. He loved speaking in public, and he loved the reactions of an audience. But Dutch enjoyed acting wherever he was. Using a broom handle as a microphone in his room, he would perform exciting play-by-play "shows" of pretend athletic events. Secretly he dreamed of becoming a radio sports announcer once he finished college.

Dutch was at Eureka College in 1929 when the Great Depression began. The entire country had money problems. Businesses had to close, and people lost their jobs and their homes. Many could not afford new clothes or food. The depression lasted for several years. During the summers, Dutch was able to work at his old lifeguard job. Yet money for school was still tight. He considered dropping out, but Dutch Reagan was not a quitter. He found work on campus as a dishwasher in the girls' dorm, and he stayed in school.

Get a Job

Dutch graduated from Eureka in 1932 with a degree in economics. His father wanted him to get a sales job in a store, but Dutch decided to follow his own mind. So he borrowed his father's old car and drove to Chicago to try to find the job he really wanted—in radio. All the big stations were looking for

▲ RADIO DAYS! Dutch's first job out of college was as a radio announcer.

someone with a lot of experience. But there was a tiny station in Davenport, Iowa, called WOC that was willing to give him a chance.

Dutch put on one of his best "broomstick" performances. He pretended that he was calling one of the old college football games he'd played in.

He was hired! Dutch Reagan, radio reporter, read everything from local news to weather reports. After a few months WOC's sister radio station in Des Moines, Iowa, needed a sports director. Soon Dutch Reagan was traveling all over the region for WHO, announcing both college and professional sports.

Radio Days

Ronald Reagan was a sports radio announcer during the 1930s. At that time, radio was America's most popular form of entertainment. Listeners could tune in to live music and comedy shows, Westerns, space adventures, soap operas, mysteries, news broadcasts, and books read on the air.

On October 30, 1938, an actor named Orson Welles (pictured above) read a radio play called "War of the Worlds." Many listeners thought Martians were attacking Earth. People ran out of their homes screaming. Others drove their cars to safety. It wasn't until later that evening that listeners learned it was just a radio play!

Listeners tuned in to hear his smooth voice. His descriptions made the events come alive.

In the spring of 1937, he went to California with the Chicago Cubs to report on their pre-season baseball games. They played not far from Hollywood. Dutch had a friend from Iowa who now made movies there. He decided to get in touch.

His friend, Joy Hodges, suggested he find an agent to help him get into movies. He made some phone calls and met an agent who got him a screen test at Warner Brothers Studios. Dutch had to wear makeup, memorize a script, and recite his lines with another actor. All the while the movie cameras were rolling. Dutch was relaxed and loved every second of his screen test!

▶ **DUTCH POSES ON THE SET** for his screen test.

You're Hired!

The studio people tried to convince him to stay in Hollywood until a decision was made. But Dutch, who had squeezed in his screen test between baseball games, had to leave. "I've got to get back to my job in Des Moines," he told his agent.

▲ THIS FAMOUS SIGN welcomed Dutch to Hollywood.

"The season opener's coming up in a few days and I've got to broadcast the Cubs' games." Reluctantly Dutch went back to Iowa the next day with the Cubs, not sure how he'd done.

Just two days later, on April 2, 1937, someone at WHO handed Dutch a telegram from his movie agent. It read: *Warners offers contract seven years ... starting $200 a week. ...What shall I do?*

Dutch wrote back immediately: *Sign before they change their minds.*

The day he left WHO, Dutch left his nickname behind. Ronald Reagan was going to Hollywood to become a movie star.

Chapter 4

Hooray for Hollywood!

The first film Ronald Reagan made for Warner Brothers was *Love Is on the Air*. He played a radio announcer! At first Ronald was nervous. But as soon as he started speaking his lines, he relaxed.

▲ A MOVIE MAGAZINE featured Ronald Reagan and Jane Wyman.

While he was filming *Brother Rat* in 1938, he met an actress named Jane Wyman. They got married in January 1940. The next year their daughter, Maureen, was born. A few years later, they adopted a son, Michael.

The Reagans made many Hollywood friends. Most of them belonged to the Screen

Actors Guild (SAG). SAG was a union that helped actors get fair treatment from movie studios. Like most actors, Ronald had to join SAG—even though he didn't want to. But once he saw that many actors weren't getting a fair deal in Hollywood, he became active in the union. Soon he was a leader of the group.

Ronald Joins the Army

Ronald's movie career came to a halt in 1941 when he was called to serve in World War II. Every soldier had to pass a doctor's exam to fight in combat. Ronald failed the eye test, but he still had to join up. He was assigned to make training films for new soldiers.

While he was with the unit, he noticed that time and money were wasted and fewer people were needed to do the work. This idea would take him on a path far from Hollywood.

▶ RONALD JOINED the army in 1941. He is shown here with Jane and their daughter, Maureen.

When the war ended in 1945, Captain Reagan returned to Hollywood, but it was harder to get good roles. It was a rough time for him. His father had died in 1941, and Ronald needed to earn more money to care for his mother. His marriage was also in trouble, and soon he and Jane divorced.

Ronald began to spend more time with SAG. In a few years he was elected its president. He also became interested in politics. As a member of the Democratic Party, he campaigned for the party's candidates running for office in California. Later Ronald campaigned for some Republicans whose ideas he believed in.

Ronald Meets Nancy

It was around this time that Ronald met a young actress named Nancy Davis. Ronald later said, "I think my life really began when I met Nancy." They fell in love and married in 1952.

The couple had two children, Patricia and Ronald Jr. Nancy encouraged her

◀ THE BRIDE AND GROOM cut the wedding cake. It was love at first bite.

► RONALD starred with a chimp in *Bedtime for Bonzo.*

husband to get more involved with SAG. She became Ronald's closest and most trusted advisor.

In 1957 Ronald and Nancy made *Hellcats of the Navy.* It was their first and only film together. After making one more movie, Nancy decided to stay home to take care of her husband and their children.

Altogether, Ronald had starred in more than fifty movies. He still had his appealing voice and his good looks. But he hadn't had a hit movie in years, and now he was getting fewer offers.

Welcome to TV Land!

Ronald also had another job during this time. He was the host of a TV show called *GE Theater*. Ronald introduced every show and acted in a few episodes each season. He gave speeches around the country for the show's sponsor, General Electric. Ronald talked about the importance of doing things without waiting for the government to do them for you. Ronald won people over to the idea of a smaller, more efficient government.

Ronald began to think about a different kind of public life. His leadership in SAG, which lasted until 1960, made it possible for him to help its members have better working conditions. He liked meeting people and trying to make a difference in their lives. Ronald thought he might run for political office. He wanted to change the way California's government was run.

When GE ended their program in 1962, Ronald looked for something to keep him busy. He was

wealthy from his days on television. His mother had died that summer, and he thought hard about changing his life.

Ronald also changed political parties. His ideas of fewer taxes and a smaller

◀ REAGAN ENJOYED campaigning for governor and meeting the voters.

government were more like those of the Republicans than those of the Democrats. By 1966 he felt he could be a strong leader—better than California's current governor, Edmund Brown. So, with Nancy's support, Ronald entered the race.

The new candidate promised that, if elected, he would make sure the state did not spend so much of its citizens' money. He said the government should not make so many decisions for the people. He believed most Americans wanted fewer laws to obey and lower taxes to pay. Ronald Reagan won the election by almost one million votes.

Mystery Person

☞ **CLUE 1:** From the time I was a kid in Austria, I was interested in bodybuilding. My dream came true when I moved to the United States in 1968 and won several important bodybuilding championships.

☞ **CLUE 2:** I started to appear in movies in 1976. I played myself in a documentary called *Pumping Iron*. Then I went on to play action heroes in hit movies.

☞ **CLUE 3:** Like Ronald Reagan, I decided to go into politics. In 2003 I won the election as governor of California.

Who am I?

ANSWER: ARNOLD SCHWARZENEGGER

Chapter 5

From Statehouse to White House

Governor Reagan was eager to begin his new job. He chose a team of advisers who shared his ideas to help him change California.

The serious issues of a state were harder to solve than problems in the movies. Most of California's lawmakers were members of the Democratic Party and didn't agree with many of Ronald's ideas. But he needed their votes to make new laws or change

◄ **RONALD REAGAN is sworn in as the governor of California.**

THE CALIFORNIA CAPITOL is located in Sacramento. Reagan had to get along with members of both political parties.

old ones. Because he didn't have any experience as an elected official, Ronald had to find ways to work with the lawmakers.

The governor had other problems to face. First he had to figure out how to save money and cut spending. So he raised taxes. He closed some state hospitals—a decision both doctors and patients fought against. He also asked state colleges to start charging students money to go to school. (Up until then California students could attend state colleges for free.)

Troubled Times

Throughout the state, angry students held protest marches. They also held "sit-ins," where hundreds of

▲ **IN 1967 POLICE TRIED TO KEEP STUDENT PROTESTERS** from becoming violent on the campus of the University of California, Berkeley.

people sat down in one spot, blocking public buildings or roads.

More protests broke out the following year. In 1968 African Americans in Los Angeles—and elsewhere around the United States—reacted with anger to the murder of civil rights leader Dr. Martin Luther King Jr. Homes and businesses in Watts, a mostly black area of Los Angeles, were burned and robbed. The streets became dangerous.

The riots made many Californians afraid. Governor

Reagan had to act quickly and decisively. He sent National Guard troops into Los Angeles. The next year he sent the troops armed with bayonets and tear gas onto college campuses, where students were protesting the unpopular Vietnam War. The National Guard finally ended the riots. Some people called Ronald a hero for ending the unrest. Others said he acted too forcefully and showed poor judgment by sending so many troops to stop the protests.

Passing Laws

But with peace restored, Ronald could turn to other business. He got laws passed to protect parklands in the state. He cut state spending so California had fewer money problems. He worked with lawmakers to cut taxes and help poor families. By the time Ronald's first four years as governor ended, he had learned how to get things done. People liked him because, when he talked, he made them feel comfortable. Many

► **CALIFORNIA LAWMAKERS look on as Governor Reagan signs a bill into law.**

Californians thought he had done a good job in moving the state forward. In 1970 Ronald ran for a second term and won.

Ronald Runs for President

The Republican Party had been watching Governor Reagan's continued success in California. In 1976 he hoped to be chosen as his party's candidate for President. He campaigned to get the nomination but lost to Gerald Ford. (Ford went on to lose the election.) So Ronald spent the next four years giving speeches around the country—keeping his name and

▲ REAGAN GAVE HIS ACCEPTANCE SPEECH for the Republican nomination for President. George H. W. Bush ran as his vice president.

his ideas before the American public.

In 1980 Ronald Reagan tried again, this time getting his party's nomination to run against President Jimmy Carter. Ronald talked about his ideas to balance the budget, cut taxes, and make the military stronger. He talked about the greatness of America's ideals and the need for a forceful leader. Ronald made strong connections with the crowds as he joked with them. He asked voters: "Are you better off now than you were four years ago?"

On Election Day they answered. Ronald Wilson Reagan beat Jimmy Carter and brought Republicans back to the White House.

Party Animals

A political party is a group of people who want to elect to office someone who agrees with their ideas.

In the United States, the two largest political parties are the Democrats and the Republicans.

In the 1870s Thomas Nast, a newspaper cartoonist, used the donkey to stand for the Democrats and the elephant to stand for the Republicans. He chose the donkey because it is strong-willed and the elephant because it is intelligent but easily controlled.

Democrats today say that the donkey is smart and brave, while Republicans say that the elephant is strong and dignified.

Chapter 6

The Reagans Go to Washington

After Ronald was sworn in to office in 1981, he and Nancy settled comfortably in their new home— the White House. All of Reagan's children, along with Moon and his wife, gathered to celebrate his

inauguration. There were dinners, dances, and lots of parties to enjoy. The Reagans looked forward to all of the great things they would be doing.

But two months later, on March 30, 1981, tragedy struck. The new President had just given a speech at a Washington hotel. As Reagan, his staff members, and his bodyguards were

▲ JUST BEFORE HE WAS SHOT, Ronald Reagan waved to a crowd of admirers.

leaving, four gunshots suddenly rang out. The President was hit. So were Press Secretary James Brady, a Secret Service agent, and a police officer. All of the men were rushed to hospitals.

Reagan needed emergency surgery. Before he was operated on, he joked with the doctor: "I sure hope you're a Republican." Even while wounded, Reagan used his humor to relax those around him.

Within weeks the President recovered. The police arrested John Hinckley, the man who shot Reagan and the others. Doctors found that Hinckley was mentally ill. He was sent to a special hospital instead of prison.

◀ RONALD AND NANCY were surrounded by their family on inauguration night.

President Reagan
survived the attack
more determined
than ever to keep his
election promises.
As governor
President Reagan had
learned how
important it was to negotiate
with politicians who might not share his views.
Reagan and his Republican supporters were

Meet Nancy Reagan

▲ NANCY REAGAN poses in the Red Room
of the White House.

Nancy Reagan was born
Anne Francis Robbins on
July 6, 1921, in New York City.
Her parents nicknamed her
Nancy. Shortly after she was
born, her father left the family.
Later her mother married Dr.
Loyal Davis, who adopted
Nancy.

After college Nancy became
an actress in New York City. A
movie studio official suggested

conservative politicians. People who consider themselves conservatives don't like having too many government rules that regulate how people live and do business. They don't like too many taxes, or taxes that they consider too high or unfair.

Many Democrats are more liberal. They believe that the government can help solve more problems than Reagan thought. The Democrats want more government programs—which would mean new or higher taxes to help pay for the programs.

As President, Reagan's easy way of communicating helped him push through many conservative ideas—including a law that greatly lowered the taxes many Americans had to pay.

◄ **NANCY REAGAN worked hard to make the Foster Grandparent Program a success.**

she try out for films. So Nancy moved to California, where she met Ronald Reagan. "My life really began when I married my husband," she has said. The actress appeared in eleven movies before becoming a full-time wife and mother.

As First Lady, she was active in the war against drugs and alcohol, as well as being in a foster grandparent program. Nancy redid parts of the White House. She was famous for the elegant, formal dinners that she gave for the world's leaders and for her fashionable clothes, which were often a bright shade of red.

▲ **BRITISH PRIME MINISTER** Margaret Thatcher and Ronald Reagan worked closely together and were friends. The two are walking the President's dog Lucky.

A Safer World

President Reagan also turned his attention to finding ways to make the world safer. Perhaps living through World War II made Reagan especially concerned about protecting America. He would spend more and more money to build up the U.S. armed forces. He wanted to create a space shield, called Star Wars after the popular movie, that would blow up any enemy missiles launched at the United States. But some Americans questioned the President. They felt his actions encouraged other countries, such as the Soviet Union, to build up their own armies and weapons supplies.

At the time, the Soviet Union was the strongest enemy of the United States. The nation was made up of many small countries that had been joined together after World War II. It was ruled by one central government, which made all the rules and decisions for its people. The communist system of government was very different from our democratic one, where Americans elect leaders and vote on laws. Reagan proposed that both countries reduce the number of nuclear missiles they had. The Soviet leader, Mikhail Gorbachev, agreed to talk.

Reagan knew that he needed four more years in office to reach this important goal. Americans gave him the chance in 1984 as they elected him to a second term.

▶ RONALD REAGAN and Mikhail Gorbachev met many times. Here they are shown in Moscow.

Reagan's Next
Four Years

Reagan wasted no time in getting down to the business of making the world safer. In 1985 he met with Gorbachev in Switzerland to begin their talks. The two leaders got to know each other and became

▲ **REAGAN AND GORBACHEV** helped bring about peace between their nations.

▲ ON A VISIT TO BERLIN, Reagan challenged Gorbachev to tear down the Berlin Wall.

friends. Their common goals smoothed the way for lessening the number of nuclear weapons.

During the talks, President Reagan traveled to Berlin, Germany, in 1987. This city had been divided at the end of World War II. The U.S. and its allies oversaw a free West Berlin and the Soviets controlled East Berlin. In 1961 the Russians built the Berlin Wall, cutting the city in two. Anyone trying to escape to West Berlin—and to freedom—was arrested or shot. The Berlin Wall was a symbol of the cold war—the struggle for power between the Soviet Union and the United States. The wall was a sign of the unfairness of the Soviet system.

Reagan gave a speech to the people of West Berlin that challenged Gorbachev to "tear down this wall!"

Jelly Beans, Mr. President?

Everybody has a favorite snack, and Presidents are no different from other hungry Americans. Ronald Reagan kept a jar of jelly beans on his desk. James Buchanan gave sauerkraut and mashed potato parties! Check out the foods some other Presidents raided the kitchen to find.

☞ **George Washington**
cream of peanut soup

☞ **Ulysses S. Grant**
cucumbers soaked in vinegar

☞ **Chester A. Arthur**
mutton chops

☞ **Franklin D. Roosevelt**
fried cornmeal mush

☞ **Dwight Eisenhower**
TV dinners

☞ **Bill Clinton**
burgers and fries

Making History

A little more than six months later, a historic day arrived. On December 8, 1987, Reagan and Gorbachev came to an agreement to reduce nuclear weapons. This treaty was one of the steps in the breakup of the Soviet Union. President Reagan had a political triumph. Within another two years, after Reagan left office, the Berlin Wall finally would come down.

Nearing the end of his Presidency, Reagan could look back at other events—good and bad. He had appointed the first female Supreme Court justice, Sandra Day O'Connor, in 1982. He had shown Americans that he could also feel deep sadness. When the space shuttle *Challenger* exploded in 1986, killing its crew, the President comforted the nation. He said, "The future doesn't belong to the faint-hearted. It belongs to the brave."

But the President also approved a secret and illegal sale of weapons to the Middle Eastern country of Iran. He had been trying to win the release of Americans being held hostage by Iran's ally, Lebanon. Some of the weapons money was also given to Contra rebels. They were trying to overthrow the democratically elected government of Nicaragua—a nation in Central America. Many of Reagan's aides lost their jobs because of the Iran-Contra affair, but Reagan stayed in office.

Reagan's second term ended in 1988. When he smiled and waved for the last time from the White House, he was an ordinary citizen once again— that nice guy with a great voice that people loved to listen to.

◄ **FAREWELL!** The President gave a good-bye salute on the day he left office. Next stop? California.

Chapter 8

Heading into the Sunset

Nancy and Ronald returned to their home in Los Angeles, California. As a retired President, experienced in national and world affairs, Reagan was comfortable as an elder statesman. He spent his time writing a book about his experiences as President and giving speeches to organizations and companies around the globe.

What most of the world didn't realize was that the former President was suffering from Alzheimer's disease.

▶ **THE FORMER** President continued to give speeches after he left office.

► **MAUREEN REAGAN and her husband, Dennis, helped Nancy care for Ronald.**

People with Alzheimer's slowly forget how to speak and eat. They can no longer understand what is going on around them. They can no longer recognize their family. Finally Alzheimer's patients must have someone else take care of all their needs. The disease is frightening for both patients and their loved ones.

A Journey Begins

Reagan shared news of his illness with the nation in 1994. He handwrote a letter that was sent to newspapers across the world, ending with these words:

"I now begin the journey that will lead me into the sunset of my life."

Nancy and a team of nurses and helpers spent the next ten years caring for him as he gradually became weaker. Nancy worked to increase awareness about Alzheimer's and called for more

scientific research into the disease.

On June 6, 2004, Ronald Reagan died at home. He was ninety-three. Across the country people mourned the President's death. His state funeral was held five days later at the National Cathedral in Washington, D.C. Crowding the service were friends from every part of Reagan's past—including Mikhail Gorbachev. Reagan was buried on the grounds of his presidential library in Simi Valley, California, that evening.

Many people admire Ronald Reagan for helping big business and shrinking government by getting rid of many costly programs. Others say these programs were needed by average and poor Americans.

► NANCY REAGAN kissed her husband's casket. They were married for fifty-two years.

But all Americans might agree that Ronald Reagan succeeded in carrying out the important mission his loyal supporters gave him long ago. He reminded people how great America could be. He helped weaken communist rule and paved the way for a freer world. These were, in the end, his finest roles.

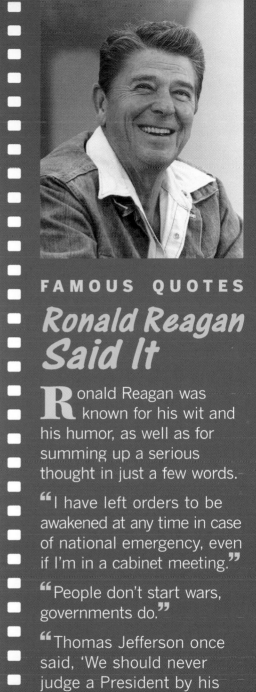

Ronald Reagan Said It

Ronald Reagan was known for his wit and his humor, as well as for summing up a serious thought in just a few words.

"I have left orders to be awakened at any time in case of national emergency, even if I'm in a cabinet meeting."

"People don't start wars, governments do."

"Thomas Jefferson once said, 'We should never judge a President by his age, only by his works.' And ever since he told me that, I stopped worrying."

"You can tell a lot about a fellow's character by his way of eating jelly beans."

Interview

Talking About Ronald

▲ Ron Reagan

TIME FOR KIDS editor Kathryn Hoffman Satterfield spoke with Ron Reagan about his father.

Q: *How do you think your father would want people to remember him?*
A: After he was shot, he felt even more strongly that he was President for a reason—to do good for others. He was a decent, honest person. That made him an attractive leader.

Q: *If he were alive today, what would he work on?*
A: He'd probably work on reducing taxes, improving peace in the Middle East, and dealing with terrorism.

Q: *What is your fondest memory of your father?*
A: Whether we were body surfing in the ocean or

swimming races in our backyard pool, we both loved the water. He'd often play touch football with me and my friends. He was supposed to be in his office [when he was governor of California], but he couldn't resist the fact that there was a football game going on with a bunch of seven-year-olds. So he'd play quarterback for both teams.

Q: *What do you find most inspiring about your dad?*
A: His personal decency. As President you're a powerful guy, and you can boss people around. But he never took advantage. He was always good to the people around him and treated them the same, whether they were mowing the lawn or they were his secretary of state.

Ronald Reagan's Key Dates

1911   Born on February 6, in Tampico, Illinois

1937   Appears in his first movie, *Love Is on the Air*

1947   Elected president of the Screen Actors Guild

1948   Divorced from Jane Wyman

1952   Marries Nancy Davis

1966   Elected California's governor

1980   Elected President of the United States

1981   Shot in attempted assassination

1984   Re-elected President

2004   Dies on June 6, in Los Angeles, California

1913 The moving assembly line is introduced by Henry Ford to build cars.

1969 Neil Armstrong becomes the first person to walk on the moon.

1991 The U.S. Women's Soccer Team wins the World Cup.